Original title:
Snow Way Out!

Copyright © 2024 Creative Arts Management OÜ
All rights reserved.

Author: Cameron Blair
ISBN HARDBACK: 978-9916-94-318-2
ISBN PAPERBACK: 978-9916-94-319-9

Solstice in Isolation

Beneath the frost, we slip and slide,
Each step a dance, with pride denied.
We build a snowman, big and round,
Yet somehow, we both fall down.

Cryptic Cadence in White

The flakes fall straight, a puzzling game,
Shapes shift and change, who is to blame?
I'll take a leap, but my coat gets stuck,
In the drifts, I'm out of luck.

Celestial Freeze

A snowball flies and hits my nose,
Laughter erupts, humor grows.
The squirrels are spies in winter's glare,
Plotting schemes from their frozen lair.

Glimmers of Ice

The world is bright, a crystal ball,
Yet here I sit, just trying not to fall.
With boots of rubber and mittens of flair,
I waddle about, no grace to spare.

The Icy Interlude

Frolicking in the icy air,
My socks are wet, but I don't care.
Slipping, sliding, a festive show,
Fell on my back, now look at me go!

The world outside is white and bright,
I build a snowman, a wobbly sight.
He asks for carrots and a hat too,
I gave him a wig, now he's a crew!

Veils of Frosty Night

The moonlight dances on frozen streams,
A penguin waddles, or so it seems.
Tripped on a branch and yelled 'Oh dear!',
My laughter echoes, crisp and clear.

Snowflakes twirl in a playful way,
Trying to catch one, but they sway.
I close my eyes and spin around,
Fell in the fluff, I'm snowbound!

Inescapable Flakes

Sledding down hills at breakneck speed,
Face full of snow, it's what I need.
Launch off a jump just for the thrill,
Land in the snow, now that's a chill!

The kids all shout with glee and cheer,
While I'm just busy building a pier.
A snow fort stands, a castle divine,
Watch out! Here comes my snowy design!

Bonds of Winter

Hot cocoa spills on my favorite clothes,
As I laugh and nibble on frozen prose.
My dog is rolling, he loves the chill,
He steals my mittens, oh what a thrill!

The fire is crackling, the night is young,
With playful puns, we've just begun.
We dance around like goofy geese,
In our own world, we find our peace.

Eclipsed by White

The world has worn a frilly coat,
I slipped and fell, oh what a note!
A snowball flies right past my face,
In this wintery, wobbly race.

My feet like sausages in boots,
Unruly snowdrifts - oh, the hoots!
A sled's my chariot, I scream with glee,
But I'm now stuck in a snowbank spree!

The Thawing Dilemma

The sun peeks out, the ice does drip,
With every drop, I lose my grip.
I made a snowman with a smile,
Now his hat's a soggy pile.

My gloves are wet; my fingers freeze,
I try to dance, but fall with ease.
Winter's grip is slipping fast,
Who knew fun could end so vast?

Lament of the Frost

The chilly breeze whispers my fate,
With snowflakes dancing; they can't wait.
A snow fort strong, or so I thought,
But now it's just an icy blot.

I dreamed of battles, heroes bold,
But freezing tempers leave me cold.
So here I sit with frozen toes,
A prisoner of weather's woes.

Caught in the Flurries

I ventured out to share some cheer,
But snowflakes swirled; oh dear, oh dear!
I tumbled down like a clumsy clown,
Waving my arms, my dignity drowned.

The dog is jumping, full of zest,
While I am now a snowy mess.
With laughter ringing loud and clear,
Winter's fun is truly here!

Barren Beauty

A field so white, a sight so grand,
With a frozen smile, it takes a stand.
But wait, what's this? A snowman frown,
He lost his nose, oh, what a clown!

In puffy coats, we waddle wide,
Shivering smiles from side to side.
Slipping here, a tumble there,
We laugh it off, without a care.

Whirls of White

Twirl and spin in frosty fun,
Chasing flakes like they're the sun.
A scarf flies high, a mitten lost,
Do we regret? Not at this cost!

With snowball fights, the giggles rise,
While icy worms give us surprise.
In the tundra's grip, we can't complain,
Just ducks in boots, in winter's rain.

Secrets of the Slush

Beneath the pile, a secret lies,
A half-eaten sandwich, oh, what a prize!
Forgotten snacks, once prized and neat,
Now mushy slides beneath our feet!

Splashes sound like fun galore,
But what's the puddle hiding more?
With slippery tales that make us squeal,
We dance through chaos, with zest we feel.

Cascading Frost

Icicles drip, like nature's tears,
We dodge them swiftly, and shift our gears.
Frosty breath in the chilly air,
What's that? A snowball? Beware!

With sleds that zoom, we race the trees,
Like runaway dogs chasing a sneeze.
Laughter echoes across the chill,
In this frosted world, we find our thrill!

Silence on the Frost's Edge

A flake floats by, just like a cat,
It lands on my nose, imagine that!
I giggle and sneeze, oh what a mess,
This chilly surprise? It's anyone's guess.

The snowman grins, his carrot askew,
His eyes made of coal, one fell right through.
Together we pose, a frosty brigade,
Yet I swear that I hear him start to fade.

The snowball fights spark up with delight,
But I slip on the ice, oh no, what a sight!
Laughter erupts, I roll like a ball,
Winter's a circus, and I'm the main draw.

As I waddle back home, frozen but jolly,
The plow cars rush, oh what a folly!
With hot cocoa dreams swirling inside,
I smile and think, I'll take this wild ride!

The Crystal Bound

Tiny crystals twirl like ballet hawks,
While penguins parade in little socks.
They slip, they slide, down the icy lane,
Chasing their tails, oh, the glorious pain!

A polar bear's hat looks snug on his head,
He thinks he's oh-so-cool, but he's really just Fred.
The icicles hang like a chandelier,
As he whispers sweet nothings, "I'm freezing here!"

The snowflakes hold meetings to plot and to plan,
On how to surprise the unsuspecting man.
With snowballs they target, without any doubt,
But oh, what a riot when they all get tossed out!

With giggles and grins, they cover their tracks,
Leaving me wondering what's next in their acts.
As the sun starts to rise, the fun fades away,
But winter's just teasing; it will come back to play!

Frosty Enigma

A flake of frost on my nose,
I giggle and dance, strike a pose.
My laughter echoes, a joyful sound,
As I tumble and roll, round and round.

The penguin's waddle, oh what a sight,
In my backyard, he's lost his flight.
He looks so confused, scratching his head,
Who knew that winter is where he'd spread?

My snowman's hat is a little too tight,
He squints in the sun, what a silly plight.
With a carrot-nose and a smile so wide,
We share a secret, winter's funny side.

I question the clouds, why so much fluff?
Did they mix up the recipe? That's not enough!
For in every flurry, there's joy to be found,
In the frosty enigma, laughs abound.

Shadows on the Snow

Footprints trailing in the white,
Squirrels skitter—what a sight!
They peek at me from the trees,
Pretending to be busy with ease.

Giggles echo on icy paths,
As snowflakes play their funny drafts.
I slip and slide, a graceful fall,
The snow covers up my winter brawl.

A snowball flies, oh what a throw,
Right past me, and into a show!
The dog gives chase, with fur all wild,
In this winter world, we're all a child.

In shadows cast, we play our games,
Filling the air with silly names.
For every tumble, there's joy to share,
In the snowy blanket, life's light as air.

When the World Turns White

When morning breaks with a dazzling light,
The world transforms, oh what a sight.
I wander out with a mischievous grin,
Adventures await as the fun begins.

Snow drifts high, an unlikely peak,
The neighbor's dog starts to speak!
With each woof, a poof of snow,
Our wonderland's here, let's steal the show.

My gloves are soaked, but spirits soar,
We build igloos and laugh, what's in store?
In every flurry, a story's spun,
Finding joy under the winter sun.

With sleds a-swoosh, we race in delight,
Through the frosty forest, oh what a flight!
As the world turns white, we find our cheer,
In this funny place, there's nothing to fear.

The Last Flake's Secret

Once a flake, now the last to fall,
Whispering secrets, its tiny call.
It twirls and spins, a ballet so grand,
Just waiting for someone to take its hand.

The children laugh, the snowballs zoom,
Every corner echoes with winter's boom.
As it cuddles close to the chilly ground,
It giggles softly, a sweet sound found.

What tales it holds, this flake so small,
Of snow-fort battles and winter brawls.
Riding on breezes, dancing with glee,
A tiny performer, so wild and free.

So when winter comes, let laughter flow,
For in every flake, there's a funny show.
Embrace the chill and join in the fun,
For the last flake's secret has just begun!

Winter's Labyrinth

In frosty mazes, I do roam,
With icy paths that feel like home.
Each turn I take, I trip and slide,
A frozen laugh, my trusty guide.

The snowflakes dance, they question me,
Why wander here, can't you all see?
But here I am, in fluffy delight,
Guided by giggles, not fright.

A snowman grins with a carrot nose,
He knows the way, or so it goes.
I ask him for directions clear,
He chuckles back, 'Just have some beer!'

So here I trudge, despite the chill,
In every flake, a laugh, a thrill.
Lost in winter's wacky charm,
With each snowball, no cause for alarm.

Shivering Horizons

The frost creeps in, it steals my toes,
I've made a friend in winter's clothes.
A jacket snug, a hat so bright,
Together we shiver, what a sight!

The sledding hill is steep and bold,
With children soaring, young and old.
I leap aboard, so full of cheer,
And tumble down, oh dear oh dear!

The cocoa flows like rivers now,
Upon my lips, it takes a bow.
A marshmallow dive, I make a splash,
In cups of warmth, my worries dash.

As stars poke through the velvet sky,
I laugh and shout, I'm flying high!
This winter scene, a playful spree,
Shivering dreams, just wait and see!

The Stillness of Snow

The world is hushed, a snowy white,
Where laughter echoes, pure delight.
My dog leaps high, his joy untamed,
In a blanket soft, we both are framed.

Icicles hang like shiny spears,
But look, there's no cause for fears.
They dangle down, just shining bright,
I dodge them all, in sheer delight.

A snowball flies, it finds my head,
'Tis a sign, the battle's spread.
A snow fort built with quirky pride,
I defend my post, with arms spread wide.

Among the stillness, joy does roam,
In frozen lands, I find my home.
With every laugh, the chill's undone,
In winter's grasp, we all have fun!

Blizzards of the Heart

When winter howls, with all its might,
My heart ignites, it's sheer delight.
I build my dreams in drifts so high,
With every flake, I'll learn to fly.

Board games spread on icy floors,
Laughter lingers through all the snores.
We huddle close, so warm, so bright,
As snowflakes whisper through the night.

The snowball fights ensue with glee,
A hilarity, a joyous spree.
As snowmen take their stand so tall,
I toss a flake, and give my all.

In blizzards wild, we play and prance,
With spirits high, we take a chance.
In every flurry, joy will start,
Amidst the chill, the warmth of heart.

Veils of Icicles

Icicles hang like chandeliers,
Catching light and winter's cheers.
But one took flight, oh what a sight,
It's now a hat for my dog, quite right!

My cat plots snowball fights all day,
While I slip and trip in a clumsy sway.
Up the gasps from neighbors ring,
As we become the winter's clumsy king!

Hot cocoa spills from numbed hands,
As we dance to winter's frosty bands.
With every slip, laughter rolls,
In these chilly, merry, snowy strolls.

Labyrinth of the Lost Flake

Once a flake fell, with dreams galore,
Now it's lost, who knows wherefore?
It sought a home on a dog's big nose,
But dashed away, oh, how it goes!

My scarf a maze, tangled in thread,
Frosty whispers swirl in my head.
Each step a risk, a twist, a turn,
In this fluffy chaos, we all learn.

The kids throw snowballs, their giggles ring,
As I dodge like a fool, it's a jolly fling.
With each flake that flutters, we all know,
In this game, it's the falls that steal the show!

Heartbeats in the Chill

With hearts racing, we dash about,
In the frozen realm, there's no doubt.
Each puff of breath, a foggy sign,
And laughter dances with every line.

My boots squeak loud, like a comedy play,
As I waddle around, losing my way.
In the midst of frost, we jump and glide,
Like penguins on ice, oh what a ride!

With mittens mismatched, we craft our dreams,
Snow angels made from giggles and screams.
In this frosty air, fun's our refrain,
Creating memories amid the chilled domain.

A Silence Wrapped in White

A blanket of white wraps the ground,
In this peaceful hush, giggles abound.
But oh, what's that? A snowman's frown,
His carrot nose is upside down!

We sprint for warmth, our faces aglow,
While jolly neighbors sport their best flow.
The scarves are flying, the hats take flight,
In this snowy chaos, everything feels right.

With snowball fights that teeter on glee,
Each throw a chance to giggle and flee.
As we build our castles, our worries unspool,
In this frosty wonderland, we all feel the fool!

The Frosted Maze

In a garden wrapped in white,
Where my dog took a fright,
He buried his nose so deep,
Only his tail wiggles in sleep.

I grabbed a shovel with glee,
Thought I'd dig a path, you see,
It turned into a giant mound,
Now I can't locate the ground!

The neighbors peek from their doors,
Laughing at my snow-filled chores,
I built a fort, it's quite a sight,
Though it's taller than me, what a fight!

Adventures lost in icy seas,
I'll leave my mark, or maybe a cheese,
As I slip and slide like a fool,
Winter's playground is my new school!

Beneath the Snowy Veil

Under blankets white and fluffy,
My cat thinks she's a little puffy,
She pounces and rolls with delight,
    Creating a snowball fright!

I thought to stack snowman tall,
But my sneaky hat took a fall,
Now it sits there, oh so sad,
Mumbling, 'This is just plain bad!'

With every step, I plot and plan,
To conquer this winter wonderland,
But I tumble, and down I go,
    Carried off by the chilly flow!

Giggles echo in the icy air,
Snowball fights turn into a dare,
With cheer and warmth in every bite,
We'll laugh till the stars are bright!

Trapped in Ice

I ventured out to make a slide,
But my feet had other plans, they confide,
Spinning like a top on freeze,
Flailing limbs, like I'm at ease!

Got stuck in the frozen stuff,
Thought it'd be easy, not that rough,
Now my boots are making tracks,
Leading me deeper into knick-knacks!

Ice cubes in my drink in the sun,
Why is this not as much fun?
I did a dance, slipped on my shoe,
Least I made a winter debut!

My laughter echoes, it's hard to hide,
In this chilly world, I've turned the tide,
Every twist and turn feels awry,
But really, who doesn't love a good try?

Silent Drifts

In a world of quiet, soft, and bright,
I lost my mittens, what a plight,
They vanished as I turned to play,
Now frostbite wishes to come my way!

Frosty flurries cover my path,
I'm not ready for this winter bath,
With every breath, a cloud appears,
Not sure if it's warmth or my fears!

I rock back and forth with grace,
As I navigate this chilly space,
Falling over, rolling 'round,
It's a spectacle; look at me bound!

But giggles rise in the winter gale,
As friends join in, we set sail,
With laughter, hugs, and hot cocoa too,
Who knew cold could feel so new?

Beneath the Quiet Cover

Under fluffy blankets bright,
A snowball fight brings pure delight.
Kids bundled up, they laugh and shout,
In the chill, there's no way out!

Sleds slide down the hills so steep,
While parents watch, they barely peep.
Hot cocoa waits to warm their toes,
But outside, the chaos only grows.

With snowmen built, they stand so tall,
Wearing hats and scarves, they know it all.
But when the sun begins to pout,
Those jolly folks might just fall out.

Fingers numb, and cheeks aglow,
Who says winter can't put on a show?
Yet, as the evening drapes its clout,
How to get home? No way, no route!

Echoes in the Cold

In winter's grip, a crunching sound,
Echoes of laughter swirl around.
Snowflakes dance on chilly breeze,
With frozen noses, they play with ease.

The igloo made, a fortress bold,
But inside - hot chocolate to behold!
They sip and giggle without a doubt,
Yet outside, they're lost - oh what a rout!

Penguins sliding, a sight so grand,
Yet each falls prone upon the land.
As they recover from their clout,
They look around - no way out!

But who can frown when fun has reign?
Watch as they hop up once again.
In this frosty, chilly bout,
The joy remains, no reason to pout!

Entangled in Frost

Twinkling lights upon the trees,
Decorations swaying with the breeze.
But stepping out, what's this about?
With every step, I'm tangled out!

Scarves that twist and mittens that slide,
Each move a dance on icy tide.
I tripped and slipped without a doubt,
The ground's too slick, I can't get out!

A snowball flies, my aim is off,
It's hit the cat, and now it's scoffed!
With laughter ringing, jokes in spouts,
The furry friend's now on the route.

Chasing giggles, sights to see,
But with each turn, they laugh at me.
Yet in this fun, there's no need to pout,
In winter's world, we're all knocked out!

Pathways of the Unseen

Footprints trace a tale not told,
Grinding paths where stories unfold.
In the dark, we seek to shout,
But winter's cover can hide us out!

With each crunch, I feel my way,
Whispers echo what penguins say.
They waddle past, stuck in the route,
What should I do? I'm lost, no doubt!

The moonlight glows on frosted glass,
Reflecting giggles as they pass.
To dance beneath the stars, there's clout,
Yet, look around - where's the way out?

But in this maze, I feel just fine,
With laughter shared, it's all divine.
For every twist and turn about,
In chilly fun, we figure out!

The Stillness of Frozen Dreams

In winter's grip, we slip and slide,
A frosty dance, we can't abide.
With every step, a comic fall,
Nature's laughter echoes, a call.

Hot cocoa spills, we laugh it off,
Snowmen wobble, oh what a scoff!
The chill bites hard, but spirits soar,
While chasing flakes, we crave for more.

A snowball flies, and battle starts,
The art of dodging, true fine arts.
Amid the laughter, we forget the cold,
These frozen moments, a joy to hold.

So take a trip where blizzards play,
In wintry wonder, we lose our way.
Embrace the quirk of icy glee,
A frosty world, come laugh with me!

Glacial Journeys

We set off brave on this slippery road,
With socks like paddles, our fate bestowed.
Each stomp a ballet, each slip a twist,
In this frosty world, we can't resist.

The snowflakes giggle, dancing down,
We wear the white like a lopsided crown.
With cheeks like apples, noses aglow,
We stumble and tumble, oh what a show!

Winter's a joker, love it or hate,
But a snowman's grin shines like fate.
As slides turn into tumbles, oh what a scene,
Each frosty adventure, a jolly routine.

So grab your mittens, come take a chance,
Join the frosted fun, slip into the dance.
In every shiver, there's laughter loud,
Chasing the chill, our playful crowd!

Frost-kissed Forks

With forks and spoons, we whisk and twirl,
A winter feast in a frosted whirl.
Casseroles freezing, pies turn to rock,
In this icy kitchen, we must unlock.

Mittens are lost, oh where did they go?
In search of warmth, we joyfully crow.
A marshmallow blizzard, a sticky mess,
Can you believe it? We're in distress!

Carrots for noses, they joke and tease,
In icy laughter, we share the breeze.
A pie crust slips, and giggles abound,
We dance through the chaos, snowflakes around.

So here's to the kitchen, our frozen delight,
With forks stuck in snowdrifts, ready to bite.
Let's toast to the fun, laughter, and cheer,
In this winter wonder, we all persevere!

Beneath a Blanket of Ice

Underneath this icy quilt, we play,
With muffled giggles, we seize the day.
In frozen fields, we create a splash,
Every tumble and roll, a gleeful crash.

Icicles dangle, nature's sharp teeth,
While snowflakes tickle, bringing sweet relief.
We craft our dreams on this glittery sheet,
A winter wonderland, a snowshoe retreat.

Grab a sled, let's race the chill,
Down the hill, we go with a thrill.
Each twist and turn brings giggles anew,
In this frosty playground, we all pursue.

So come and wander 'neath this ice,
In winter's embrace, life feels so nice.
With laughter united, let spirits take flight,
Beneath this cap of frost, we shine so bright!

Confinement in Cold

Locked indoors, a flake parade,
With scarves and hats, we are arrayed.
Mugs of cocoa, marshmallows rise,
While snowmen plot their frosty lies.

Sleds now serve as living room chairs,
In this fortress, no one cares.
We'll dance with shadows, laugh and prance,
Stuck in this wintry, wild romance.

Outside the window, a snowball fight,
But here, we're cozy, warm, and tight.
We trade our plans for board games still,
In this chill, a heart may thrill.

The flakes may fall, but I won't fret,
In our snug blanket, I'll never regret.
Adventure calls in dreams we weave,
In this frosty hold, I won't leave.

Ethereal Silence

Hushed whispers float on the icy breeze,
The world wrapped in bunches of snowy fleece.
We hum tunes of pine trees, tall and grand,
While critters dance, in silent land.

Time ticked slow, like molasses run,
In our winter palace, we're never done.
Each flurry, a giggle, each drift, a tease,
In this quiet, we find our ease.

Letting winter's whimsy be our muse,
We craft our dreams, and freely choose.
Ponder the universe with cocoa in hand,
In the stillness, we make our stand.

Though frosty vines may bind our feet,
The chill can't stop our merry beat.
Together we snicker, together we beam,
In this ethereal calm, we live the dream.

When the World Stilled

The world outside turned into fluff,
As cheeks turned rosy, winter's tough.
Giggling fit to burst at the seams,
In fluffier dreams, we laugh and scheme.

Boots get stuck, a slippery chase,
With snowballs tossed in a giddy race.
Our breath, like steam, fills the air,
Each chilly moment, we gladly share.

The neighbors grumble, the roads are lost,
But in this blizzard, we count the cost.
Of fun and laughter, snowflakes' delight,
We'll keep warm through this frosty night.

When the world stilled, it came alive,
In silly antics, we truly thrive.
So bring on the blizzard, let it roar,
In our cozy chaos, we crave for more.

Boundless Winter

A blanket of white, a fluffy sea,
Where elves and gnomes play hide-and-seek.
Hot s'mores by the fire, tales to spin,
In the great embrace of a winter din.

We fashion giants from sparkly snow,
With carrot noses, they steal the show.
Chasing our laughter beneath the gray,
In this boundless winter, we seize the day.

The jingles of laughter, oh, what a treat,
As kittens tumble with frosty feet.
Yet here we stay, so snug and warm,
With winter's charm, we revel in the storm.

So let the chill nip at our toes,
In this endless winter, anything goes.
We'll dance and twirl with rosy cheers,
As love and warmth conquer the years.

Frozen Labyrinth

In the land of icy twists,
We wander with frosty fists.
Every corner looks the same,
And I tripped over a snowman's frame.

Lost my mittens, what a plight,
Chasing snowflakes that take flight.
I shout for help, but it's all in vain,
Just a squirrel laughing at my pain.

Where's the path? I seem to stray,
Got sidetracked by a snowball play.
Thought I'd conquer this frozen maze,
But I've been here for endless days.

Now I'm stuck, a frosty clown,
With icicles hanging from my gown.
If you find me, please don't pout,
Just throw some hot cocoa about!

Whispering Winds of Winter

The wind howls with a shiver,
As I slip down a frozen river.
My sled's a rocket, here I zoom,
And crash right into the neighbor's broom!

Giggles echo from the trees,
Snowflakes dance, they tease and freeze.
Laughter bubbles up so bright,
Even the icicles seem polite.

Chasing shadows through thick flurries,
Every step's an icy flurry.
I take a leap and lose my shoe,
Winter games, who knew they grew?

With a slip and a slide, I twist and twirl,
Like a frozen ballerina, watch me whirl!
But as I laugh and spin about,
I realize now, there's no way out!

Chilling Escape Routes

Plotting paths in a snowy plot,
But my sense of direction's caught.
I took a turn, I lost my map,
Ended up in a penguin's lap!

Frostbite fiends and chilly glares,
Countless snowballs fly through the airs.
I dodge and weave like I'm in a race,
Then find myself stuck in a snowdrift's embrace.

I spy a sign for hot chocolate treat,
But my feet are frozen like concrete.
In this winter maze, I dare to shout,
Has anyone found the way out?

But laughter rings in the snowy knoll,
As warm thoughts bubble in my cold soul.
Though escape seems quite a lot,
I'll take this fun, like it or not!

Frostbound Traces

Footprints lead on a frosty spree,
With my pants now stuck to the tree.
"Merry Christmas" turned to "Help me, please!"
As I fight to free my shivering knees.

The ground is slick, like slippery soap,
Thought I'd fly, but I can't cope.
Each step I take, I slip and fall,
I should've brought my ice skates, after all.

Snowball fights on this frosty stage,
But I'm entangled in a winter cage.
They pulled the snowman right on my head,
Now I'm a chilly giant, full of dread.

So if you hear a muffled shout,
It's just me, stuck with no way out.
But in this freeze, I find delight,
Laughter warms this frosty night!

Haunting Frostbite

Cold fingers dance, they twist and twirl,
My nose is red, like a cherry swirl.
A ghost on ice, I glide and slip,
With every fall, I lose my grip.

The chill will creep, it's plotting schemes,
It gnaws at toes, and steals my dreams.
But laughter echoes on the frost,
In this skating rink, I'm never lost.

Bundle me up, I say with cheer,
Each tumble's worth a hot cocoa near.
With friends so dear, we take a shot,
At slipping, tripping, but all for naught.

So here's my pledge, to all out there,
If we must freeze, let's do it fair.
A joyful shiver, a frosty grin,
In icy madness, let the fun begin!

The Last Flake

I waited long for the flurry's rise,
But now one flake's a sad surprise.
It dances down, a little boss,
I catch it quick, the albatross.

Tiny and white, it melts away,
In coffee hot, it couldn't stay.
With every sip, a gusty sigh,
The last of winter, but oh, my!

I pat my cheeks, then poke my chin,
It's just chilly, where to begin?
My hat's too snug, my scarf's a beast,
Yet here I stand, my joy increased.

The streets are slick, my feet, they dance,
A slip, a slide, it's winter's chance.
A single flake's a faded joke,
Yet in my heart, the laughter woke!

Reflection in Ice

In the pond, I see my face,
A frozen grin, a silly grace.
The world looks back, a caricature,
In frosty glass, I seek the cure.

My cheeks are bright, my eyes enthralled,
Yet ice beneath, it's a slippery brawl.
I flap my arms, but oh, what luck,
I'm dancing now, like a clumsy duck.

Every slide's a comedic show,
As winter whispers, "Yup, let's go!"
With laughter loud, I step with glee,
The icy mirror reflects me free.

So glide with joy, and let things sway,
In this fun freeze, we'll laugh away.
A smiling face on frosty glass,
In every slip, may joy amass!

The Winter's Grid

Frosty paws with mischief bright,
I plot my course, a zigzag flight.
The sidewalks draw a web of fun,
As I navigate, who'll be the one?

A dance of feet on a snowy sheet,
I twirl and spin, oh what a feat!
But then I trip, a grand retort,
A stellar fall in my slick support.

The grid's a trap with quirky bends,
Yet I can't stop; I'd rather pretend.
Each slip a laugh, each slide a win,
In my winter quest, let the fun begin!

So join the map of laugh install,
A whimsical tour, where we might fall.
Together we'll play, in this icy vibe,
Life is a grid, let's now imbibe!

The Frigid Frontier

On the roof, a penguin sings,
While a squirrel does some silly swings.
Ice cubes tumble from the sky,
As snowmen dream of flying by.

Frosty hats fill up the street,
With snowballs pitched like candy treats.
Slipping kids with rosy cheeks,
Chasing giggles, oh the peaks!

Cocoa flows like rivers wide,
While jackets shrink and mittens hide.
Laughter dances in the air,
As icicles hang like drawings rare.

Who knew winter could be so bright?
With frosty fun, we lose all fright.
Join the freeze, the zany crowd,
In this frosty wonderland, we're loud!

A Retreat in White

In a cabin high on a frosty hill,
Where cocoa's warm and hearts can fill.
A raccoon wears a cozy hat,
While snowflakes flicker, just like that!

Sleds whistle down the snowy slopes,
Crash landing laughs, and then the hopes.
Hot boots landing, what a weight,
As snowmen make their lumpy fate.

Penguins dance, their flippers thrash,
As children slip and make a splash.
We twirl in yards, as snow drifts gleam,
What a winter wonder, what a dream!

Frosted breath in the chilly air,
As we leap like deer with flair.
When winter calls out for a play,
We answer loud, hip-hip-hooray!

Companions of the Cold

In thick, warm layers, we all gather,
With goofy grins and plenty of blather.
Building forts that touch the sky,
Where snowball battles always fly.

Chasing down a rogue snow dog,
Caught in antics, we laugh and slog.
Mittens tangled, we're a mess,
But in this chill, we feel so blessed.

Seeking warmth from cookie trays,
Our fun continues through the craze.
A dance of flakes upon our nose,
In this white world, our bright joy grows.

So gather friends, let winter cheer,
With snowy shenanigans, have no fear!
In frosty grips, we laugh and shout,
Oh what a world, with no way out!

Lured by the Winter Glow

Glowing lights adorn the trees,
As joyful laughter rides the breeze.
The warmth of friends, the sparkle bright,
Chasing snowflakes, oh what a sight!

A toasty fire crackles loud,
As we parade among the crowd.
In fluffy boots, we stomp around,
Making merry in our winter playground.

Snow-topped hills call us to race,
Round and round we twist and trace.
With frozen noses, joy ignites,
A flurry of giggles under bright lights.

Though chilly winds may whip and whirl,
Our winter fun is quite a pearl.
So come and play without a doubt,
In this frozen realm, we've maxed out!

Winter's Icy Embrace

Fluffy flakes descend with glee,
Turning the ground to a white sea.
Sleds fly high, kids squeal with cheer,
Watch out for mom, she's coming near!

Boots slip around in a festive dance,
Even the dog thinks it's a chance.
When hot cocoa spills on your lap,
Laughter's the best, it's a cozy trap!

Snowmen rise with buttons and carrot,
They look so jolly, not a hint of sorrow.
But one looks sideways, what a stance,
Did he catch my double-glaze glance?

Frosty weather, oh what a ball,
Twisting and spinning, we make the call.
To stay inside or brave the chill,
Whipped cream beards, we laugh until!

Crystal Maze of Silence

In a world where whispers freeze,
Footsteps quieted, oh what a tease!
The trees like giants wrapped in white,
Welcome us all, what a charming sight!

Giant snowflakes, nature's confetti,
Let's scatter them, our hands get sweaty.
Each step a puzzle, a wobbly quest,
Tripping over drifts with unwelcome zest!

Snowball fights break the calm,
Chilled cheeks bring us all a balm.
A slip, a slide, down a frosty hill,
Laughter echoes, what a thrill!

In this maze of glistening light,
Every corner hides an icy fright.
But giggles burst like bubbles in air,
A world of wonder, frosty and rare!

Drifting Through the White

Pillows of snow on rooftops high,
A blanket cozy to the eye.
Chasing the clouds that float so slow,
With every step, the laughter will grow!

Snowflakes drift like tiny dancers,
Catching our breath, hapless prancers.
Frosted noses and rosy cheeks,
In this winter wonderland, all it speaks!

Hats go tumbling, scarves take flight,
Wind chimes jingle in pure delight.
As we gather the flakes for a new dream,
Watch them vanish like vapor, it seems!

The world transformed in a chill embrace,
Every corner a white-coated space.
Let's sip on laughs that never cease,
In this frosty magic, suddenly, peace!

Shimmers of a Hidden Path

Under the moon, the night sparkles bright,
Illuminating paths in the frozen white.
Footprints lead to mischief and fun,
Where laughter lingers long after it's done!

Fuzzy mittens on tiny hands,
Building igloos, our secret lands.
Chasing shadows that play on snow,
Every twist and turn, come join the show!

Hot chocolate stands waiting near,
Marshmallows melting, fill with cheer.
Each sip a giggle, a sweet retreat,
We dive back in, our hearts want to beat!

The path ahead glimmers like stars,
The cold can't stop us, not even wars.
For in this frosty, whimsical land,
We're kings and queens, snowballs in hand!

Echoes Beneath the Snow

In a flurry of white, I made a mound,
A snowman with a carrot, but he's falling down.
He waved at a sledder who flew past my way,
And said with a grin, 'I'm just here for play!'

The dog loves the flakes, he leaps and he bounds,
Chasing all the snowballs that end with loud sounds.
But just like his joy, the snow's here to stay,
We'll giggle and tumble, in this winter ballet!

With mittens that match, I slip and I slide,
My boots are quite soggy, oh, where's my pride?
The cold bites my nose, but I can't seem to frown,
For laughter erupts, as we tumble and clown!

So here we dance 'neath the frosty grey sky,
Making snow angels, oh me, oh my!
The echoes of winter are filled with such mirth,
In this chilly wonderland, we discover our worth!

Winterbound Whispers

Under blankets of white, we whisper and shout,
About how to escape, but there's really no route.
The snow's piled up high, like a fluffy white wall,
We're stacked like the cookies that we drool over all!

Hot cocoa is brewing, with marshmallows afloat,
I dropped one in surprise, it danced like a boat.
We giggle at snowmen with crooked little grins,
With hats that are frozen and noses from bins!

The cat stares in horror, it's just not her scene,
Darts through the door—she's no winter queen!
Yet here we are frolicking, with glee in our heart,
In this winterbound comedy, we're all playing part!

So let the snowflakes fall, so soft and so bright,
We'll build forts and nap 'til the stars fill the night.
With laughter and joy, this blanket we sow,
In a love story written in winters of snow!

A Chill in Time

The clock strikes the hour, but time's lost its way,
We're stuck in a winter wonderland play.
While others are rushing, racing about,
We're making grand snow forts, or flopping about!

Frosty flakes tumble, they tickle my nose,
My friend just got stuck in a very deep pose.
He mumbles, "I'm okay!" but I laugh till I ache,
As he wiggles and shimmies, it's all a great fake!

Sleds zooming down hills, we cheer as we crash,
Each fall is a victory, a jubilant splash!
We might not be graceful, but who needs that flair?
When laughter is louder than the cold winter air!

So raise up your glasses of sweet cocoa warm,
Let's revel together in this chilled little charm.
Though a chill may come, we embrace what we find,
In this frosty time warp where joy is aligned!

Elysium in White

In a realm covered white, our mischief unfolds,
While building a mountain of powdery gold.
A snowball brigade, all aimed at my head,
I dive for the ground as I dream of my bed!

Flakes drift and flutter, like feathers in flight,
We giggle and squeal at the marvelous sight.
But one rogue snowball made its cheeky debut,
Now I sport an icy crown, oh what a hullabaloo!

With everyone laughing, I'm stuck in a mound,
While visions of snowmen are swirling around.
"Hey, can you lend me a hand?" I shout with a grin,
They roll in the snow, "You look like you win!"

Yet up I pop up, with laughter so bright,
In this Elysium where our joy takes flight.
The cold may surround us, but warmth's within reach,
In this light-hearted heaven, it's laughter we preach!

Winter's Grasp

Winter creeps in, a slippery friend,
With frosty toes, it just won't end.
Sleds crash and tumble, laughter does soar,
Hot cocoa spills, oh! What a chore!

Icicles hang like nature's art,
Snowmen wobble, they fall apart.
Kids in jackets, looking so round,
Whirling and twirling, falling down!

Fortresses built with determination,
Become soft piles in a harsh situation.
Gloves are soaked, but spirits are high,
Let's sled again, oh me, oh my!

Snowflakes dance, but why do they bite?
Chilled to the bone, I flee from the fright.
Yet in this chaos, joy will prevail,
Winter's mishaps tell the best tale!

The Chilling Entropy

What's that noise? Was it a bear?
Nope, just me, lost in mid-air!
Trying to ski but I twirl and spin,
Landing headfirst in a heap of skin!

Gloves stuck together, hat askew,
Why did I think this was a good view?
Slipping and sliding on a serious spree,
A dance with fate, they all laugh at me!

The igloo's a palace, so cold yet grand,
I lost my way to the warm, dry sand.
Winter, you tease, with your frosty breath,
You make me shiver, but also laugh 'til death!

And though the chill wraps me like a quilt,
I'll brave the chill, my courage built.
Laughing at penguins in their silly waddle,
Together we glide, oh, let's all straddle!

Refuge Beneath White

Buried treasures beneath white sheets,
A lost muffin, and my warm feet!
Under this quilt, so soft and bright,
Who needs a plan when this feels just right?

Shovels and sleds become our toys,
In vast snowlands, we're just girls and boys.
Where's the park? Oh, lost in a drift,
A snowy cave, is this life a gift?

The roof's sagging, can it hold this weight?
A bird said, "Yo, it's one big plate!"
Winter's buffet, it's truly a dream,
Meals served warm, where smiles beam!

So let's build castles, with turrets so high,
Jane saw a dog and was ready to cry.
Laughter erupts as we tumble and roll,
In this frosty wonderland, it's good for the soul!

A Tundra's Story

Adventure awaits in a white wonder,
Every step crunches, oh, the thunder!
My boots now wedged in a snowbank deep,
It's a game of hide and seek, not sleep!

The wind whispers secrets of chilly fun,
Yet my nose is red, oh, look at that sun!
Snowballs a-plenty, they fly in the air,
One lands square, now I need repair!

With scarves wrapped tight, oh, what a sight,
Snowflakes falling like stars at night.
Yet here I stand, looking quite silly,
Getting hit again? Oh dear! What a filly!

But wait! There's laughter, it's filling the space,
As we stumble and giggle, we embrace this race.
Winter's antics may cause us to pout,
But my friends, without you, I wouldn't get out!

Veils of the Frosted Horizon

The flakes are dancing with delight,
While penguins are sliding, quite a sight.
They're trying to glide and to race,
But bump into trees, oh what a face!

Hot cocoa spills like a wild spree,
Sipping while snowflakes tickle the knee.
An igloo contest with wobbly walls,
Which one will topple? Oh, the downfall!

Cats in sweaters, feline fashion show,
Paws slip and slide, look at them go!
A chase for the yarn, they dive in the snow,
Pouncing on snowmen, their true foe!

Bags of candy canes on the floor,
Kids slide around yelling, "Give us more!"
With giggles and laughter, we cheer and shout,
Is there any party when it's all out?

Frozen Pathways

Ice skating on a pond, what a fear,
Children tip-toeing, giggling near.
One little slip and down they go,
Landing in snow with a face full of glow!

Sledding down hills, oh what a trip,
Faster and faster, let it rip!
Racing with friends, who will prevail?
But off course, someone veers on a trail!

The dog dashes through puffs of white,
Rolling in snow, such a silly sight.
Snowballs being thrown with a hearty cheer,
No one is safe from this frosty sphere!

The winter sun sets with vibrant hues,
As chilly evenings bring out our views.
Pillows of snow on rooftops take flight,
And laughter echoes in the frosty night.

Whispers of Winter

Chattering teeth, laughter is loud,
Around a fire, wrapping in a shroud.
Stories are told, as embers glow bright,
But the marshmallows stuck - they're quite a sight!

Snowmen like giants, all lopsided and round,
With carrots for noses precariously found.
But wait, what's that? Did it just blink?
Or was it just Bob's attempt to rethink?

Hot chocolate fights, what a fine mess,
Splashing across, it's pure happiness.
As cups get filled for another round,
Who knew that sweetness could come unbound!

In cozy corners with blankets to share,
We laugh at the wind and the chilly air.
Winter whispers of tricks and delight,
With comical tales that stretch through the night.

Chilled Solitude

Skiers zoom past, like lightning on ice,
Lost in their thoughts, isn't that nice?
But wait, one who forgot how to steer,
Calls for help as he flies with a cheer!

Penguins waddle, briefcase in flippers,
Late for a meeting, upon icy zippers.
His boss is a seal? What a cruel fate,
A conference call to contemplate!

Frosty fingers, buttons are hard,
But the snowball fight calls, my most heartfelt card.
An avalanche starts from a playful throw,
Who knew two cousins could steal the show?

As the night falls, the quiet surrounds,
Footsteps are muffled, no vibrant sounds.
But in this calm, there's laughter awake,
In chilled solitude, friendships we make!

Shadows of a Snowstorm

The flakes fell fast, a fluffy fight,
I can't see where I'm going tonight!
I tripped on a drift, oh what a scene,
Do I walk like a human or a penguin in between?

My neighbor's snowman has a crooked grin,
I swear it's aiming for my chin!
The path is a maze, I feel like a fool,
As I slide past my yard, like a kid on a stool.

Dressed in layers, I waddle like a seal,
This winter fun, is it even real?
But laughter erupts with every slip,
How many hot cocoa cups will I sip?

At the end of it all, I look like a mess,
But who would trade this winter's jest?
With each blustery puff, I chuckle and shout,
In this frosty land, there's no way I'm out!

Frosted Footprints

I ventured outdoors, boots laced tight,
But the icy ground gave me quite a fright!
Step by step, I'm a dancer on ice,
Wobbling and shaking, oh isn't it nice?

Each footprint I leave tells a silly tale,
Of slipping and sliding, I could not prevail.
The welcome mat's lost beneath the white,
Now it's a game of hide and seek tonight!

Strangers all laugh as they pass me by,
Like a cartoon character, I don't know why.
"Look at that fellow, it's quite the show!"
I tip my hat, then tumble, oh no!

In the midst of my fall, laughter rings clear,
I laugh at myself, no traces of fear.
For in every slip, there's a joy to be shared,
In this frosty ballet, we're all unprepared!

The Winter's Embrace

Wrapped up tight like a Christmas gift,
Sledding downhill, oh what a lift!
My cheeks are rosy, my laughter loud,
As I zoom past a gathered crowd.

The snowball fight brings out my glee,
I launch one at Tim, but it hits me!
Covered in white, like powdered dough,
Just call me Frosty, but please don't throw!

The dogs chase their tails, a flurry of fun,
Chasing snowflakes 'til the day is done.
With mittens that sog, I can hardly clap,
But giggles escape as I stumble and flap.

When night rolls in, all cozy and warm,
A hot drink is my winter charm.
As dreams of this season dance in my head,
I'll plan for tomorrow, let's get out of bed!

Icy Entrapments

The driveway's a slide, a glistening spree,
Each step feels like a life on a spree!
I make my way with a cautious glide,
But my plans take a turn, as I start to slide.

Two squirrels are laughing, I swear it's a joke,
While I flail and flap like an old worn cloak.
The snowdrifts rise higher, I can't see a thing,
Should I build a fort or dance like a king?

A plow rolls by, with vengeance it goes,
But it leaves me to battle, what no one knows!
The wind takes a snap, the cold bites my nose,
Maybe hibernation is what winter chose.

In the chaos, joy finds its way,
Through frozen laughter, it's a wintry play.
Despite all the tumbles, I can't help but shout,
Who knew this chill could bring so much clout?

Serpentines of Silence

The flakes are swirling, what a scene,
I can't find my car, it's the biggest routine.
Chasing my dog, he thinks it's a game,
While I slip and slide, it feels quite the same.

Neighbors in pajamas, building a hill,
They're yelling, they're laughing, it's quite the thrill.
A snowball surprise, they launch with delight,
Just watch for your hat, it may take flight.

Giant snowmen with carrot noses,
Who knew that winter breeds so many poses?
Yet under all layers, I start to sweat,
That's the last time I'll embrace winter, I bet!

As nightfall creeps, we gather for cheer,
Hot cocoa in hand, I forget about fear.
Together we giggle, warmth spreading near,
With a snowman army, we conquer the year!

Artistry of Cold

Painted with frost, my yard's a delight,
The world becomes canvas, our brushes take flight.
Snowflakes are artists in shimmering white,
Transforming the mundane into pure dreamlike sight.

I watch kids tumble, crafting a fort,
So grand and so fierce, it's a winter resort.
Until one brave soul shouts, "Let's take a chance!"
And suddenly everyone's caught in a dance!

A snowball whizzed by, my hot cocoa's a loss,
Oh, what a tragedy! But wait, the gloss!
I see the laughter, the joy, and the fun,
Winter's not winter without a good run.

So we stake our claim on this frosty terrain,
With giggles and tumbles, we never complain.
Artistry abounds in this cold, crisp air,
Each moment together, a treasure we share!

The Hearth's Refuge

Outside the winds howl, an icy parade,
But here in the warmth, all our fears fade.
The fire is crackling, we roast marshmallow,
As laughter erupts like some silly callow.

A cat in a blanket, oh what a sight,
He's plotting to pounce on the flickering light.
We dive for our snacks, in this cozy retreat,
While winter's outside throws a big snowy sweep.

We tell silly stories, some make us groan,
Like the one with the penguin who wished for a throne.
But everyone chuckles, it's clear to us all,
The best sort of laughter ignites every hall.

So let the world freeze, outside thick and gray,
Inside here we're warm, in our own playful way.
With cups overflowing and hearts set to glow,
We'll take on the winter, and put on a show!

The Frozen Frontier

Out there where the chill feels like biting sled dogs,
We brave the cold, in our woolly warm clogs.
Adventure awaits on this frozen expanse,
Where snowball fights start—the wildest romance!

Each step is a mission; watch out for the fall,
One slip on the ice, and we all lose control.
But with every tumble, we can't help but laugh,
All in the spirit of winter's rough craft.

The trees wear their coats made of thick fluffy white,
Twinkling with lights, oh what a sight!
Families bundled up tight in the dusk,
We're building a world of snowflakes and husk.

So here's to the frosty, the slapstick and play,
To memories made in this ice-bound ballet.
We'll dance through the cold as if on a spree,
In this wild frontier of winter's decree!

Escape to Eternity

In a drift so deep, I can't get free,
My sled's a boat, oh woe is me!
The hills are steep, the slopes divine,
Yet here I sit, like a stuck porcupine.

A snowball fight with a frozen foe,
Strategic plans? I'll never know!
I slip and slide like a clumsy fish,
Justice is sweet, with each snowy swish.

The sky is gray, the world is bright,
I dream of sunshine; what a sight!
But for now, I'll jump and play,
In this winter wonderland ballet!

Snowflakes fall, like globby glue,
I built a man, now he's a goo!
I'll take my chance, take one last spin,
And hope my laughter leads me from within.

Layers of Silence

In fields of white, where whispers play,
I trudge along, it's quite the day!
My boots are heavy, my spirit light,
Each step I take, a comic sight.

Trees wear coats of frosty cream,
I've lost my hat, it's quite the theme!
I yell for help, but it's just a hare,
Who's busy chewing without a care.

The sound of crunch, the air so chill,
I drift on clouds, I climb up hills.
But when I fall, it's not with grace,
It's a tumble-weed in a snowy race!

With every gust, the silence breaks,
Snowy giggles, and belly aches.
I laugh so hard, I start to cry,
In this land of white, I could surely fly!

The Frozen Threshold

A door of ice, how can it be?
Is winter playing tricks on me?
I bang and clatter, I twist the knob,
The door just laughs, it's quite a blob!

I try to bribe with cookies sweet,
But all it does is shake and creak!
I grab my scarf, give one last shove,
And through the frost, I fly like a dove!

The world outside, a blinding light,
I dance with icicles, what a sight!
My cheeks are red, my breath a cloud,
In this chilly zone, I'm feeling proud!

But now I'm stuck, can't find my way,
Lost in laughter, it's here I'll stay.
To summer dreams I bid adieu,
For fun in frost is my favorite view!

Chasing the Wind

With mittens thick and nose aglow,
I sprint outside, let's see how far we go!
The wind gives chase, it tickles my face,
In this frosty bliss, I find my place.

Snowflakes whirl like dancers bold,
As frosty tales of winter unfold.
I wiggle and woosh, get caught in a flurry,
With laughter and joy, I'll never worry!

I leap and bound, a snow-filled spree,
But oh dear wind, will you catch me?
I twirl and swish, a sight to see,
In this chilly race, it's just pure glee!

My cheeks are frozen, my joy so warm,
In this parka of fun, I find my charm.
I'll chase and be chased, all day till night,
In this whimsical world, everything feels right!

Milton Keynes UK
Ingram Content Group UK Ltd.
UKHW020818141124
451205UK00012B/639